© **Copyright** – Tiarna Combs 2022

All rights reserved

This book or parts thereof may not be reproduced in any form, stored in any retrieval system, or transmitted in any form by any means—electronic, mechanical, photocopy, recording, or otherwise—without prior written permission of the publisher. All rights reserved.

This Music Manuscript Belongs To

Contact Details:

Telephone:

This Sheet Music Manuscript Paper is ideal for both professional and new learner Musician.
Suitable for students, teenagers, children, and qualified musicians, ideal for college and school.

For practicing piano, guitar and other musical instruments.

The musician's notebook dimensions and content is made up of:

- 12 Staves per page with space in between for lyrical notes
- Delightful attractive cover
- 115 pages
- Size dimensions 8.05"x 11"

Examples Of Sheet Music for Beginners

The Grand Staff.

The Grand Staff is the treble clef and bass clef joined together, with a brace at the far left side.

The Bass Clef and Notes in the Bass Clef

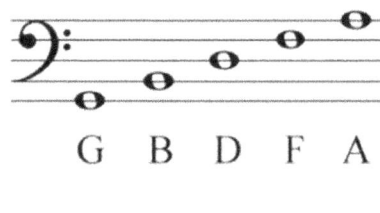

G B D F A

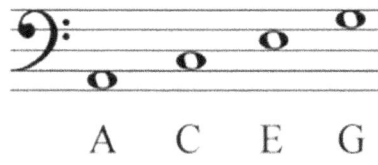

A C E G

The Bass Clef also contains 5 lines and 4 spaces in it, and each of these lines and spaces has a specific note that is located there.
The notes on the 4 spaces are A, C, E, & G.
The notes on the 5 lines are G, B, D, F, & A.

Say the note names on the Spaces going from the bottom to the top several times.
Then do the same thing with the notes on the Lines,
again going from the bottom to the top.

**With acknowledgements and thanks to instructables.com

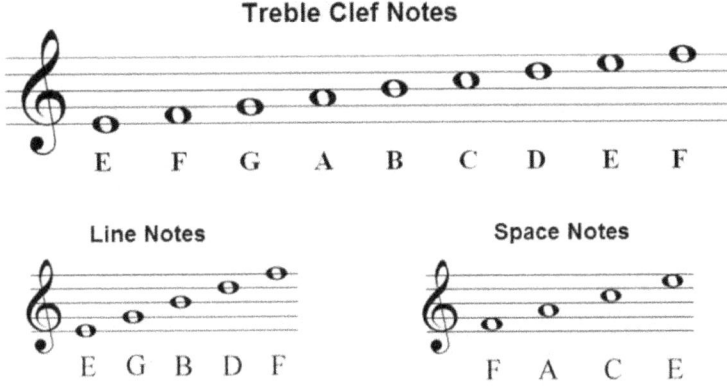

The Treble Clef contains 5 lines and 4 spaces in it,
and each of these lines and spaces has a specific note that is located there.
The notes on the 4 spaces are F, A, C, & E.
The notes on the 5 lines are E, G, B, D, & F.

The Grand View of All Notes on the Lines and Spaces in Treble and Bass Clef

Here you have all of the notes on both the lines and spaces in each clef, for easy review.
Take some time to read each note in each clef, and then try to look away and name all of your Space notes in each clef or all of your line notes in each clef.
Keep doing this each day until you can name the notes without looking at any hints.

**Remember to say in the beginning whether the note is on a line or on a space, as this will help reinforce that information in your brain and your fingers when you play it on the piano.
** Remember also, to always learn your notes from the bottom line or space to the top line or space in the clef that you are working in.

www.ingramcontent.com/pod-product-compliance
Lightning Source LLC
Chambersburg PA
CBHW081231080526
44587CB00022B/3893